Drawing Words

poems by

BARB REYNOLDS

Finishing Line Press
Georgetown, Kentucky

Drawing Words

ACKNOWLEDGMENTS

Grateful acknowledgment is made to the editors of the following
publications where these poems, some in earlier versions, first appeared:

Apogee Journal/Queer Folio: Ash
Bookbaby.com/Isolation Journal, Volume One: excerpt from The Good File #1
Breakwater Review: Underbelly of the False Ballet
Finishing Line Press/*Boxing Without Gloves*: Arithmetic, Drawing Words
From Whispers to Roars: Ice
Marin Poetry Center Anthology 2020: Enough
POEM: A Huntsville Literary Assoc.: Hunger, The Library, Safety in Numbers
Streetlight Magazine: Marco Polo

Publisher: Leah Huete de Maines
Editor: Christen Kincaid
Cover Art and Design: Carol Ehrlich
Author Photo: Irene Young

Order online: www.finishinglinepress.com
also available on amazon.com

Author inquiries and mail orders:
Finishing Line Press
PO Box 1626
Georgetown, Kentucky 40324
USA

Table of Contents

First, there is memory.
Then, the mechanics of remembering.

~Jude Nutter
March 2003, and My Father Remembers the War

DRAWING WORDS

If it happened at night, we wrote words
in the dark on each other 's backs
with our fingertips in our best cursive ever,
guessing each letter in a whisper
as it was drawn; the more elaborate

the better. Stifled sounds of whacks
and pleas jammed the air quelled
inside that long hallway. They forgot
that even though our door was closed,
we were still on the other side; we heard ,
we heard.

Here, my turn. You wrote slowly, curled,
and I concentrated so hard to follow
the upswing of your *f* and the downward
bend to the next letter. We picked bigger
and bigger words: *crayon* or *monster*
or *dodgeball.* I didn't know how
to plug my ears and draw words
at the same time; I had to keep starting over.

The next morning, even if we'd known
what to say, Mom's eyes forbade it. A rug
was moved to cover a stain. We picked
at our oatmeal. A silence echoed, louder
than a scream in a tunnel.

TRIGGER

You pointed at her face
with a steady hand. Pulled
the trigger

with us watching. Click
of the misfire
halted my breathing.

Our stepbrother, almost
seventeen, reached
for the jammed

pistol, never breaking
the stare. I couldn't
understand

how he took it
to your friend
down the street

instead of clearing
the chamber
and blowing you away.

Kids, go back to bed,
someone ushered,
monotone

& prodding.
We crawled obediently
into our bunks,

pulled the weighted
covers of dread
over our bodies.

She slept
in the play room,
knife under her pillow.

ICE

When I hear ice clinking in a glass
I think of my mother and how we could tell,
by slur or by gait, if she'd had one drink

or two-and-a-half; how, by the third, a chill
would coat her in a hardened shell,
or she'd rain down like hail with tearful

stories we'd heard before. I'd call around
to the usual bars when I was ten, long after
dinner, long after bedtime. I'd check

to make sure she was breathing
when she slept, ribs rising & falling
in slow frigid waves. But there are no

middle-of-the-night rantings now,
no shaking us awake from our splintered
sleep, making us get up

to wash dishes we'd left in the sink.
No calls from jail now as some guard
listens in, the click and static filling

the fissure between us. We drift, broken
chunks of lost glacier. We slide away,
cubes released from their frosty silver trays.

MERCY

In elementary school, Eve & I were in the *gifted program*,
which meant, we were pulled out of class twice a week
for special testing. Each time Mrs. Walker motioned

for me to go, I'd get up from my front-row seat, schoolmates
laughing & pointing as I walked down the skinny aisle
between desks & out the door- then again,

when I returned. We were already the family
with the cops at our house a few times a year
when the blows wouldn't stop, and mom told my oldest sister

to call. They'd step inside, see mom's bloodied face,
three kids huddled and peeking. They'd say to dad,
Cool it, don't go too far-then saunter out,

handcuffs still shining in their holders.
As dad raised his hand more at home, I raised mine
less and less at school. By junior high,

I was sitting in the back, saying the answers in my head,
becoming invisible. I'd avoid teachers, and eventually
they stopped calling on me. It felt like mercy.

SOLDIERETTES IN OUR PARENTS' WAR

We were a shiny filigree
of hard-won medals,
on a good day. Other days
we were bartered burdens,
vexations, little mirrors
they could barely look into.
We learned to step lightly,
step where they didn't, step
over trips like a minefield.
We learned silence, the art
of looking downward.

THE GOOD FILE (#1)

Every few months, Mom would pick us up
after work in her Bonneville and we'd drive
through *Taco Pronto*, eat back home
around the kitchen table, all of us
unwrapping warm, crunchy tacos
from their crisp yellow paper. Orange sodas
in cold bottles with straws. Then we'd play *Tripoley*
or watch *Room 222*, together.

*

I'd water down her vodka & gin when she was at work.
My oldest sister would yell at her to stop drinking. But Eve
stayed quiet, just pulled out a joint one evening
as we sat at the kitchen table, mom three drinks in.
I thought she would flip out when Eve said
You get high your way, I'll get high mine
and lit it, held it out. Mom almost tried it.
After that, I left her bottles alone.

*

In high school, Eve won an award from the American Legion
and as we took our seats, they came high-stepping down the aisles
in fringy white uniforms and hats, clapping in circles,
like they were clanging cymbals in some imaginary marching band.
I was first to lose it, then Eve got going. Mom tried to scold us
but as the clapping got louder, she caved, shoulders shaking.
How we howled together on the way home.

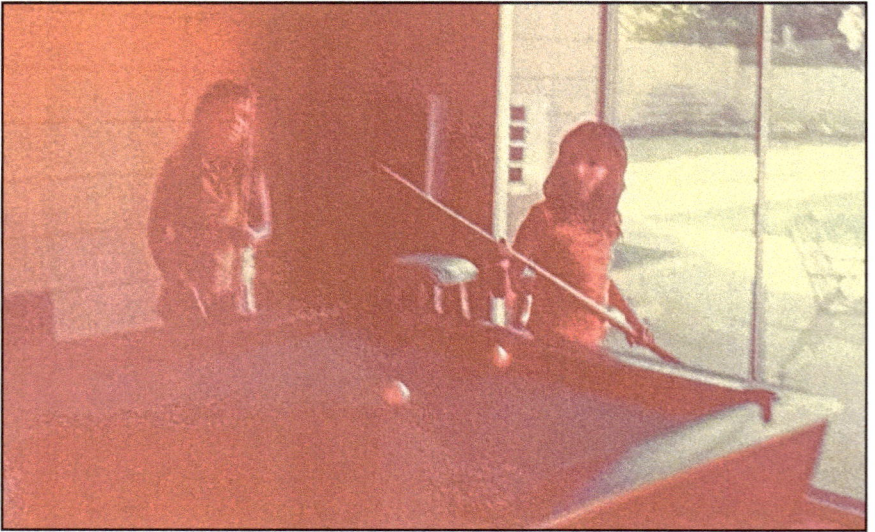

PHOTO: PLAYING POOL AT NINE & TEN

We're at our dad's house. I'm holding my cue left-handed,
surveying the table, while Eve stands to the side waiting
her turn. He taught us the rules & etiquette for eight-ball

and he was serious: *No slop, forfeit your turn. Keep one foot
on the floor at all times. Don't horse around and distract
your sister.* We carry those tenets with us today. In this sepia photo

I am so slight, born two-months premature and still catching up—
ribs show through my shirt, arms thin as the stick I'm holding.
Small but mighty. Klutzy but determined, my sister still says.

Looks like I just placed the cue ball after her scratch, set up
a bank shot that'll come back & sink a solid behind the line.
Even then, the methodical one, the slow planner, while she

takes no time to look and bend and shoot, mostly getting them in.
Raised in a household of mines & pitfalls, we survived
like bunker-mates with an unbreakable devotion. *Irish Twins,*

our mom dressed us alike and everyone called us *The Girls.*
A few years after this photo, riding my skateboard alongside
Eve on her blue ten-speed, a pebble jammed my wheel

and I flew off, breaking my right arm. Eve circled me on the ground,
laughed every time she went around. I laughed too, and cried,
and walked the rest of the way home carrying my board.

She rode beside, reminding me how I had already broken
my left arm at four when I fell off my tricycle, and the shiner
I got at two, falling on my face in the yard. Much safer, pool.

Only real dangers are not packing a tight rack, tearing felt
on the break, and avoiding the eight
until it's time.

HUNGER

In the 70's, Eve and I marched
for civil rights, gay rights, the ERA.
We marched against war, hungering

for peace somewhere. Our mother
never knew-she was committed
to her own cause: to see just how far

she could disappear into a glass
every night. I did blame her then,
how we faded to the edges, starved.

But when I was outed in high school
by my best friends, I appreciated
the value of knowing how to disappear.

A couple times in 12th grade,
Jane Whitley & I walked four blocks
to my house at lunchtime and drank

screwdrivers from my mother's bar.
Then we smoked a joint
and went to 5th period History, our secret

rebellion. My mother surrendered
to a prison of gin and bills, children
& vodka- her disappointments beaten

into my morning eggs every day until,
at seventeen, I left. It would be decades
before I'd push back the plate.

SAUSAGE LINKS

I can 't smell a sausage link without thinking
about those Shriner pancake breakfasts
we were dragged to with dad in the late '60's—
slick white men (no blacks allowed)

with their grabby hands, polyester plaid pants,
red fezzes with their tassels, dangling. Too interested
in their brethren's daughters. As we moved
down the buffet line, dad added a sausage link

to my plate of scrambled eggs & pancakes,
and it touched everything. I picked around
the sausage but eventually he'd point to it and push
the plate toward me, which meant *Eat it, now.*

I sat between my older sisters at a checkered picnic table,
legs swinging, while dad slapped backs and *heh heh heh'd*
to some joke nearby. It was the only time we (over)heard
how proud he was: *Oh yes, great girls, piano, milk monitor,*

top of the class. Fake as this sausage forced down my throat.
Wrapped neatly in a smooth, tied-off casing, yet filled
with handfuls of rot. I'd hold my breath, take the smallest
bite, then drink two gulps of orange juice until the sausage

was gone. On the drive home he'd yell, quiz us
in math or vocabulary, his big blue boat of a Cadillac
floating down the 101 doing 80. If we didn't answer
fast enough he'd shout *Oh, any idiot could figure that out!*

glaring red-faced in the rear-view. I'd say to myself,
I must be an extra-special idiot then, and believe it,
and lay down on my sister's lap trying not to get carsick.
What pawns we were made to be. What inevitable

losers. Mom used to say, *Your father was such a charmer until the ring went on the finger.* It's true, I watched it every time: so gallant & funny, man of the hour, then how he'd turn.

UNDERBELLY OF THE FALSE BALLET

At the epicenter of our ballroom
the floorboards were dying to split open, against
the grain. But we needed the floor,

and by then we'd learned to *dip* and *plié*,
échappé and *pas de deux*. Bone grinding wood
grinding nail. In this family, it was dangerous

to talk about things out loud; the desperate stampede
back to equilibrium. So, we rewarded the dance,
encouraged it, even. No one wants to see

the ballerina trip and fall, collapse
under her tutu. Watch the lace, not the cracking
beneath her; watch the twirling and spinning, the smile

cemented on her face. *Those* were the lessons
we sat for after school while our friends took piano
and tuba. Even now I feel the barre rising

and I can't afford to jump that high any longer—
always having to be ready with safety nets and Plan B's,
a chenille cushion under the trick floor.

FRENCH LESSONS

Les Duponts arrivent dans une heure!
Eve says out of the blue as we pack
our father's house, mimicking our French
lessons from forty years before.
I respond on cue: *S'il te plaît, Maman, encore cinq minutes!*

We were eleven, twelve, when weekly lessons
with Frédéric began. *Frédéric, le sadist,*
I might have called him under my breath.
Or, Fred, Fred, pain in my head.

Once, when I didn't do my homework,
Frédéric ordered me to hand-copy
the entire lesson book by the following week.

I copied that book, even drew in
some of the illustrations. When I handed
it over proudly, he tore it in half
without a single glance.

My sister goes off script: *Quelquefois,*
mes enfants, la vie n'est pas juste.
And I laugh back, *Ah oui, je sais bien!*

THE GOOD FILE #2

When he was in a good mood, he'd call me *Barbles*,
wink, reach over and rub my cheek. When I had a cast
on my arm I was *Wingy*. If one of us had a cold,

we were *Sniffles*. Once, when he was in a super-
good mood, he walked in & said *Hey there, sweet stuff*,
sat down and read the paper, like the most monumental

thing hadn't just happened. It ignited a part of my heart
that hadn't been touched and I could hardly take it
in. Still, unable to hold back a smile,

I'd bathe in the warmth of that moment, let it fill
all of my deserted places. Sometimes a side of dad
came out that was so tender, like the monster

was on a quick break out back. When I played viola,
ran track, sang in the school choir, he showed up.
Every *Parent Night*, every graduation. First

to call on birthdays, often at 6am, he'd belt out
every word of the song, send a funny card,
sign it *Daddio*.

PREEMIE

I joke and say
I was a preemie
because Eve
couldn't wait
for my good
company

but the truth is,
dad punched mom
more than once
and after enough
slamming around
she spit me out,
no longer able
to bear the child

he named after
his girlfriend
at the last second,
the one he took
to Hawaii instead
of her, or at least
that's what she
told me one night
at the table-

now, how cruel
can you get,
to make her look
at me every day
& be reminded-

and just to think,

I could have stayed
inside for two more
months, floating
warm in a muted
pool, still wanted,
still a possibility.

SAFETY IN NUMBERS

Sort, like an abacus,
your broken pearls
from her ruined shells.
It's so hard to tell them apart.

Place into manageable piles
his inherited contradictions
and her inherent unease,
the things that kept you,
for all of your young years,
suspended in a hammock
of distress, swinging
between their trees.

Divide the pros of his leaving
by the cons of his staying,
never forgetting the ratio
of desertion to eviction,
or the infinite amount of peace
brought on by his absence.

Still, worry touches everything.

But there is no universal formula,
no Order of Operations
to apply here, working left to right,
brackets for stability. No safe equation
to reason out the family data.

Subtract the years she was vacant,
barely breathing, from the ones
you forfeited trying to revive
the wrong body.

ASH

Eve and I would drive to Malibu
in her midnight-blue Camaro,
sit on the sand at sunset.
I'd bring my guitar, or we'd stay silent,
hurl our dreams out onto the water
as hard as we could.

One night we came home—Mom,
drunk in the living room.
As I got closer, I saw my black
hardbound journal in her hands.
She'd read it, taken her pen to it:

We've never had a QUEER
in the family before!
Circling and underlining things.
You're SICK!
Drawing arrows, pointing.
You need a psychiatrist!!

She read sections aloud
as I nearly hyperventilated.
She asked why I couldn't be more
like Eve. If she only knew.

I burned it. Every single page,
and the cover, too. As if fire
could incinerate her hatred,
or mine. As if fire could reduce
her words to ash.

MRS. KIRK

She must have been seventy
when she started taking care of us.
White-white hair, the way her head

tremored a little, so many wrinkles.
Eve remembers a Texas drawl
but I can no longer place the sound

of her voice-only that it was calm.
When we came home from school,
cookies and milk waited & we'd play

Crazy Eights or *Go Fish* before homework.
She'd let us sip a sweet, creamy spoonful
of her coffee, our secret; let us slide

down our polished slate hallway in thick
white tube socks before mom came home.
We'd get a running start and surf for yards

until wide grout lines slowed us down.
Mrs. Kirk lived with us during the week
in a big bedroom at the other end of the house

and every Friday afternoon for five years
her son Rogers would pick her up
in his white Buick, bring her back on Monday.

My heart broke a little every time she drove
away. Years later, mom took us to visit.
We'd never been to her home, had no idea

where she lived. Eve remembers a row
of shacks with thin walls that weren't insulated,
where migrant field workers lived. I remember

how it felt on the inside: walking through
her small sunlit kitchen, running my fingers
over cracked blue counter tile, an embroidered

tablecloth in the corner; how we sat
under a tree in her backyard,
ate figs with cream.

MEMORY

When
I
ask
my
sister
to
remember
for
me

it'sbecausemybrainwassojammedwithfearworryangstdespairbackthen

that   I   didn't   have   space

                            to   retain   more

          than   the   hazy   edges

                    of everything

else

ARITHMETIC

A sudden flash, almost a dream:

> We were young, my two sisters and I, performing
> for our parents' guests, lined up on the flagstone hearth
> in a descending row, hair pulled back into matching
> flowered barrettes, hands at our sides.

I ask Eve if she remembers what we were singing back then
and she says we weren't singing at all-we were reciting arithmetic:

> *Four plus four is eight, eight plus eight is sixteen...*
> *sixteen plus...*

The recollection swirls my stomach:

> I was the youngest, trying to keep up. Felt squirmy
> but couldn't fidget, that would disappoint. My toes
> cramped in shiny black shoes & I wanted the grown-ups
> to stop staring at us with their drunken party smiles.

> *...Sixty-four plus sixty-four is a hundred twenty-eight...*
> *five-hundred-twelve plus...*

How does the mind sequester such things?

> I remember that flagstone: it ran up the wall
> to the high white ceiling and I'd scale it for fun
> and jump off, scale it & jump. Climbing the walls —
> a dry run for getting out.

THE LIBRARY

Stories were not read aloud
there; tomes of muffled
manifestos stuffed
our bookshelves. Pages torn

& stuck together, bound
by loyalty, fear; by the silence
inherent in forcing confidences.
Secrets lined the hems

of our flowery dresses,
filled our kickballs and balloons,
sewed our mouths shut.
But when at last the spine breaks,

as it must after holding for so long,
glues lose their stick, bindings
unravel. Threads stretch & pull free
from pinholes poked through

ink-stained parchment. Papyrus
and palm leaves finally let go
their dusty stories, now,
into your hands.

MARCO POLO

The rumbling would surge up
from underneath the white shag
carpet. His first insult hurled
with that infuriating smirk,
ice clinking in highball glasses,
the falling sky.

What else could we do
but escape to the pool, *our* pool.
Dive in to that muting, time-stopping
water, our deafening water.

We'd give each other a side glance
and we were off- sprinting barefoot
across the prickly lawn, just ahead
of the inferno burning up behind us.

We'd start the deep inhale two strides
before leaping, arms and legs punching
air, crashing into the deep end.
You could almost hear the *sizzle*
as we broke water. We'd stay under,
eyes closed, arms outstretched, seeking
and being sought.

Eventually, we'd find each other -
it's hard to swim away quickly
when you're giggling.

When it was time,
we would emerge as robotic
as synchronized swimmers.

ENOUGH

I gave them my childhood because I had to;
half my adulthood, their echoes in my head.
He'd pound blind fury if her expression changed,
pummel if her tone faltered. When she divorced him

she partied like a prisoner, freed. Sometimes
she'd pass out on the couch after dinner, TV blaring,
and I'd circle back every hour to make sure
she was still breathing. Even at eight

I was on patrol. At eleven, court-ordered visiting
at dad's, my sister & I tried to eat dinner-
but that familiar crying out, a sound so visceral,
so Pavlovian, I can 't hear it without intervening.

I put down my fork & headed to the kitchen,
all five feet of me, jacked up on so much rage.
As I rounded the corner, I saw him holding
his third wife by the collar of her housedress,

slapping her face back & forth, back & forth.
I ran at him like a linebacker, his eyes widening
as I got closer. Elf to giant, child to ogre, I pushed
him off her, and pushed, and pushed, until,

with my final shove, he fell against the wall
and actually slid down, like in the movies. I stared
at him- all splayed out, bully on his back-
and me there, shaking, with my newfound power.

TRAIN STATION, ITALY

At seventeen, summer after graduation,
I went backpacking with my sister
through Europe. We slept one night

under a train station awning in Florence,
waiting for the 6am to Rome. It was raining
and she had a cold. An officer walked over-

I could hear him approaching for the longest-
boots smacking wet pavement.
When he reached us I lay still,

but when his leg sprang forward to kick
Eve in the back, my hand shot out to block him,
as if I'd been trained for that move

all my life. I can still feel the leather of his boot
against my palm. I looked up and held his stare;
held his shoe mid-air. My eyes burned

as if to say *Make one more move
and I'll kill you.* Hell, my eyes probably said
Give me a reason, because he walked away.

THE NOTE

After my father died, I found
a handwritten note in the back
of a bottom drawer in his office.
It was from my mother in 1955.
She said, *Yes! Yes! I'll marry you!!,*
her flowery script all swept up
& ecstatic, and I remembered
the story of how they met:

he'd wait in line at the bank
where she was a teller, let people
go ahead until her window was free.

She went on: *You make me so happy!*
and ended with *I can't wait!!*
Exclamation points like sealing wax.

My heart sank, because I never
knew her that way;
because by the time I arrived,
all she couldn't wait for was divorce.

I sat back in his swivel chair,
even tried to inhale her perfume
from the letter, but all I could smell
was my father's musky after-shave
everywhere in the house.

ODE TO TERROR

You were a fourth sister, an angel
overseer, watching us from inside
a shadow, claiming us with a devotion
I'd never known. You woke us
in the morning, cold and holding;
walked us to school no matter the weather;
packed yourself into our lunch bags
between the sandwich & cookies, inside
the neatly folded napkins
we used to wipe our silent mouths.
0, Great Teacher! How you helped us
stay awake & aware, a vigilance
I honed down to a shiv and still carry
in my pocket. You saved us
a front-row seat for every boxing match.
Except there was just the one boxer.
And the one being boxed. You made sure
we were swaddled each night,
not in warm cotton but in your stiff coats,
like straitjackets. 0, Blocker of Synapses,
Jammer of Circuits, Warden of Words!
How you so cleverly kept us from speaking,
like the lips of dolls sewn shut
with crooked little stitches. Your love
was a cocoon, a bubble, and I floated
through this world half-here, half-gone,
insulated in your ether.

THE GOOD ENDING

Eve looks into the camera—
this is my favorite
moment of the video—
and says, *Sister, Sister:*
look where we are, and look
where we came from.

GRATITUDE

My heartfelt thanks to:

EVE REYNOLDS
GENE REYNOLDS
ANN REYNOLDS
JUDE NUTTER
ALISON LUTERMAN
ELLEN BASS
AMANDA MOORE
JANET JENNINGS
KEN HAAS
SIÂN KILLINGSWORTH
BONNIE MCMANIS
KATHLEEN MEADOWS
RON PARKER
KATHRYN JORDAN
WHIT SCHWEIZER
PENELOPE THOMPSON
SAMANTHA WALLEN
DEVIKA BRANDT
SUSIE BERG
MARGARET H. WAGNER
NAN SEYMOUR
PAMELA DAVIS
MICHELLE LATVALA
MARTINA JONES
IRENE YOUNG
CAROL EHRLICH
LOUISE KIRK
CAROL BERMAN
LORI BROWN
MAUREEN MURPHY
AMY WESTON
AVA CHARNEY-DANYSH

Barb Reynolds spent 22 years as an emergency response child abuse investigator. Her first chapbook, *Boxing Without Gloves,* was published by Finishing Line Press in 2014. Barb was a finalist for the 2019 and 2020 Joy Harjo Awards, and she is a Pushcart Prize nominee. Barb founded the Second Sunday Poetry Series in Berkeley, CA.
www.barbreynolds.com

Eve Reynolds stayed in Los Angeles and became an architect. When she is not building something fabulous, she is sketching, gardening or throwing a house concert.
www.arcolution.com